The Sparrow Who Became King of The Jungle

By Mlangeni Barrett

The Sparrow Who Became King of The Jungle

First published in Great Britain by Mlangeni Barrett in 2023.
Email: mlangenibarrett@gmail.com

Text copyright © Mlangeni Barrett 2023

All Rights Reserved

No part of this publication may be reproduced, distributed, or transmitted in any form or by any means, including photocopying, recording, or other electronic or mechanical methods, without the prior written permission of the publisher.

The story, all names, characters, and incidents portrayed in this book are fictious. No identification with actual persons (living or deceased), places, buildings and products is intended or should be inferred.

Conditions of Sale

This book is sold subject to the condition that it shall not, by way of trade or otherwise, be lent, resold, hired out, or otherwise circulated without the publisher's prior consent in any form of binding or cover other than that in which it is published and without a similar condition including this condition being imposed on the subsequent publisher.

ISBN: 978-1-7384045-0-6

Dedication

The authors dedicate this book to their families, friends and to all the little sparrows who believe that "they can."

Long ago, in one of the many great jungles of Africa, the time had come to decide who would become the next King. The King ruled over everyone and everything in the jungle. There was much excitement, but there was also a little fear in the jungle too.

All the previous Kings of the jungle proved that they were very brave. The current ruler, the Lioness became the Lioness King by defending the jungle against those who wanted to bring harm and danger into the jungle. Since she became King, nothing bad had happened in the jungle. Before the Lioness, there had been the Great Elephant King. He became King by leading all the animals in the jungle to safety during the great jungle fire.

But it was now time to choose the next King. Would the next King become as great as the Lioness? Who would take her place? *Could* anyone take her place? Choosing the next King was going to be a very difficult task.

The great Lioness King called a meeting. Every animal in the jungle was expected to attend. There had been rumours circulating around the jungle for weeks that the Lioness King was looking for a successor to take on the role of King of the Jungle. Now the time had come.

All the animals gathered before the Lioness King. She sat on her hill, looking at the excited, but anxious animals standing before her. She looked splendid with her golden crown. She roared and stared into the distance and then made her announcement.

"My time as King is ending. I have served my duty to this jungle for a long time. Someone else must now rule." She then paused and stared into the crowd. "Who amongst you has the strength, the courage and the wisdom to rule and protect this jungle?"

The Lioness King had already decided that the fairest way to find the new King was to hold a competition. The winner of the competition would take her place and lead the jungle as King. The competition would be a test of strength and courage.

There had been much discussion in the jungle about a great storm that was expected to arrive in a few days' time. All the animals had sensed that a great storm was coming. The Lioness King looked at the animals before her and announced: "The competition will be a test as to who can survive the storm. To win this competition and to become King, you cannot run away. You cannot seek shelter. You must face the storm and survive."

At the front of the audience was a little brown sparrow. Her parents had lived in the jungle all their lives, and so did their parents before them. The little brown sparrow knew nothing about life outside the jungle. This jungle was her life, but she was the only animal who was not excited by the Lioness King's challenge.

The Lioness King walked away from her hill and left the audience of animals discussing the competition. Some thought the Lioness should think again about stepping down as ruler, others bragged about their strength and that the next ruler ought to be them. But the little brown sparrow walked away slowly from the crowd with her head bowed down.

A snake called Sipho saw sparrow slowly walking away. Sipho asked the sparrow why she looked so sad. "I am sad because I want to win the competition. I love this jungle and I know that I could become a great ruler; but how can I survive the great storm? I am small and the storm will send me crushing against the towering mountains and hurt me. I am sure of it."

Sipho sighed, "Sssss. You know what I do when I have a big problem, or if I am scared about something?" hissed the snake. "I talk to the wise owl. She always has solutions for every problem, big or small." The sparrow thanked Sipho with a little smile and at once she went into the jungle in search of the wise owl

The sparrow was curious. This was not the first time she had heard about the owl's wisdom. Could the wise owl help sparrow with her fear?

The little brown sparrow flew from tree to tree in the great big jungle in search of the wise owl, but she could not find the wise owl anywhere. Discouraged, the little brown sparrow sat on a tree branch. She thought she was stupid for thinking that she could become King. How could she become King when she was so small?

Suddenly, in the distance, the sparrow heard the hoot of an owl. Excited, the sparrow flew towards the sound. The more the sparrow flew, the louder the sound of the owl's hoot. Then, the little brown sparrow saw the wise owl, sitting on the branch of one of the tall, grand old trees of the jungle.

There were many animals in the jungle that believed these old trees were very important because the trees knew all the jungle's secrets. However, the trees only revealed these secrets to the King of the jungle and wise animals like the wise owl.

The sparrow was full of joy when she finally saw the wise owl. She flew onto a branch placed just below where the wise owl was sitting.

The wise owl looked up from the book she was reading and stared at the sparrow with her big eyes. "Yes, little one. How can I help you?". The sparrow looked up at the wise owl and in a cheerful voice, said, "Hello wise owl. Sipho the snake told me that you could help me. I have a big problem."

The little brown sparrow's happiness at finding the wise owl suddenly turned to sadness. "Wise owl. How does someone as small as me show courage and bravery against the big mighty storm that is due to come? I want to be king, but I fear that the great storm will crush me against a mountain."

The wise owl was silent for a moment. She closed her big eyes and took a deep breath. Then, suddenly the great wise owl cleared her throat and gave out a loud chuckle. "Oh, my little one. Life has many storms, and we must face them all."

The great wise owl chuckled again, but louder this time. "You must believe, then believe again, and finally, believe, little one." The wise owl continued to laugh, but the little brown sparrow was confused. She could not understand why the wise owl was laughing. The little sparrow was not amused.

Then the great wise owl flew from her branch and sat next to the little brown sparrow. The wise owl stopped smiling and frowned. She looked at sparrow directly into her eyes and said,

"First, you must **ALWAYS** believe in yourself."

"Second, you must understand the storm. You see little one, if you can rise above the storm, the storm will carry you. Never ever fight the storm but learn to ride it and rise above it."

The sparrow was listening to every word. She closed her eyes and started to imagine herself flying through the storm. She was gliding. It was so easy. She felt brave and fearless.

The great wise owl continued. Her voice was stern and serious, "The last thing you need is courage. Courage comes from believing that you can do anything, and you can, my little one. You must believe in yourself; you must understand the storm and you must find your courage. If you do not do these three things, you will never become as great as you are meant to be."

The wise owl started smiling again, hooted and quickly flew away.
"Thank you, wise owl," whispered the little brown sparrow as she watched the great wise owl fly off further into the jungle.

It was late and the sparrow was far from home. But the words of the wise owl sang loudly in the little sparrow's head while she flew. As the sparrow was nearing home, a strong, powerful, wind was starting to blow. Could this be the great storm? "It could not be," thought the little sparrow. No one had expected the storm to arrive for another few days. The sparrow could feel fear rising within herself. She started repeating aloud the words of the great owl.

Believe in myself,
Rise above the storm,
Ride the storm,
Have courage

The little brown sparrow could feel the power of the storm beneath her wings and the storm pushing her forward faster and faster.

Believe in myself
Rise above the storm
Ride the storm
Have courage

The little brown sparrow opened her wings and raised her body upwards. The wind was carrying her higher and higher beyond any height she had ever flown. She rode the wind and let it carry her.

Then, the wind suddenly stopped and there was silence.

The little brown sparrow was high up above the clouds. She felt a confidence she had never felt rise within herself, and the little brown sparrow said to herself proudly, "Yes I can." She felt happy, content, and brave as she made her way home.

Three days passed, but on the fourth day, the sound of the wind grew louder and louder. Much louder than the day sparrow had met with the great wise owl. This was the great storm everyone had feared. It was finally here, and the wind was blowing strongly through the jungle trees. All the animals of the jungle gathered before the great Lioness King sitting above them on her hill. The competition had begun.

The sparrow waited for the storm, silently repeating to herself:

Believe in myself
Rise above the storm
Ride the storm
Have courage

The mighty storm arrived in the jungle bringing heavy rain and winds. Most of the animals either ran, crawled, swam, or flew searching for shelter. But the sparrow was amongst the few animals who stood and faced the storm. Then, with a determined look on her face, the little brown sparrow with her body aiming upwards and her wings wide open, flew towards the eye of the storm with no fear.

The heavy winds of the storm took sparrow higher than she had ever imagined flying, it carried her above the tallest mountains. She rode the storm and felt courageous and brave.

The storm lasted for many hours, but not once did the little sparrow let the wind and the heavy rain defeat her. She kept on rising and flying towards the lightening as it thundered and roared its heavy roar in the dark, night sky.

The little brown sparrow powered her way with ease through the heavy clouds. Then, as she flew from the storm, she emerged into bright, warm sunlight. The storm was over. The clouds had disappeared. She could eventually see the oceans below and everything in front of her, far and wide. With joy and pride the little brown sparrow flew back towards the jungle.

On her return, the little sparrow was met by the sounds of celebration. She was the happiest bird alive because she knew she had been brave and had shown courage. The great wise owl stood proudly with the other animals as the sparrow flew toward them.

With gratitude and pride, the little brown sparrow bowed at the feet of the great wise owl and thanked her. Sparrow then saw Sipho the snake and thanked him too.

It was exactly at that moment when the little brown sparrow became King of The Jungle.